15 Walks from Keswick

Paul Buttle

Published by

amadorn

Also by Paul Buttle

The 12 Best Walks in the Lake District

Fifteen Walks from Ambleside and Grasmere

Short Walks in the Keswick and Borrowdale Area

Short Walks from Ambleside and Grasmere

and

A Walking Tour of Lakeland

First published in May, 1989 as 'Ten Walks from Keswick'.
Reprinted July, 1989, September, 1989, April 1990
Expanded to '14 Walks from Keswick' May, 1991
Reprinted February, 1992
Expanded to '15 Walks from Keswick' November, 1992
Reprinted May, 1993, September 1994, August 1996, February 1998, July 1999, August 2000, (with revisions) June, 2002, June 2003, May 2004, July 2005, March 2007, February 2008, (with revisions) June 2011 and October 2012.

ISBN 0 9513717 5 4

© P. Buttle 1989, 1991, 1992, 2002
Published by Amadorn, 18 Brewery Lane, Keswick, Cumbria.
Typeset by An Údar, 18 Greta Villas, Keswick, Cumbria.
Maps by Gelder, Much Dewchurch, Herefordshire.
Printed by Ferguson Print Ltd., Keswick, Cumbria.

CONTENTS

INTRODUCTION

The fifteen walks in this guide present a wide choice of walks from modest low level walks to very challenging high level walks. Probably not all the walks in this guide will be of interest to everyone, but hopefully most people will find six or seven that are.

Categories of walks.

I have grouped the walks into three broad categories; low level, intermediate and high level. These grouping tend to be a little arbitrary - especially when the highest "low level" walk reaches over a thousand feet. All low level walks should be well within the capabilities of even the most modest walker. Four walks I have described as being "intermediate" by which I mean they are not quite as arduous as a substantial fell walk. Again this is a subjective assessment. A novice fellwalker may find them challenging enough. The four "high level" walks come well within the description of being major fell walks.

Order of walks

I have ordered the walks, at least within each category, as much as I could judge, by the amount of effort required to do them. Thus the easiest walks come first and the hardest last. This way of ordering the walks I hope will serve some purpose in helping you to decide which one to choose.

Timing of walks

This is always difficult to judge as it depends not only on an individual's fitness but also on his or her predilection for taking breaks. The 'Suggested times' in this book therefore are just a rough guide. They are calculated using a version of 'Naismith's rule':- one hour for every three miles covered and one hour for every thousand feet ascended. This way of calculating the time of a walk does not allow for any stops and picnics. If you are prone to engage in these diversions you should, of course,adapt the suggested times accordingly.

Choice of Map.

A map is essential on the fells and even on low level walks it is best to be with one. The Ordnance Survey produce two types of maps that can be used with this guide:-

Landranger Series Sheet 90, scale 1:50,000

and

Outdoor Leisure Map English Lakes, scale North West sheet: scale 1:25,000.

For low level walks the Outdoor Leisure Map is certainly the best one to have. Its large scale makes it remarkably detailed - even the boundaries of fields are represented A minor 'fault' with this map, however, is its confusing representation of footpaths and rights of way.   This arises because rights of way are represented with prominent thick green dashed lines. This is fine when these rights of way exist as footpaths but occasionally they do not exist as paths at all. More reliable are the faint black dashed lines, which don't stand out as well. These lines represent footpaths which are not rights of way. Their representation of existing footpaths, though, is remarkably accurate and surprisingly comprehensive. Sometimes, however, even these black lines fails to represent pathways which are perfectly distinct on the ground.

Unfortunately the North West sheet does not cover the start of the Blencathra walk (walk 13) this is covered by the North East sheet, and part of the Glaramara walk (walk 14) is also not covered by this map, this is covered by the South West sheet.

Safety on the fells.

I have aimed this guide more towards the aspiring rather than the experienced fellwalker. Both categories of walker, however, should ensure they are properly equipped. Ensure you have:-

- a waterproof or windproof outer jacket
- sturdy boots with a good sole pattern,
- hat and gloves
- spare warm clothing,
- a comfortable day sack
- food and something to drink
- a compass, torch and whistle.

Also be aware that weather conditions on the tops of fells can be quite different to weather conditions at lower levels. To check on Lake District weather conditions phone 0844 846 2444.

Updates.

It is the fate of all guide books that they need updating - stiles become gates: metal gates are replaced with wooden ones: some footpath signs disappear. The author of this guide welcomes being made aware of such changes. Please email:- *buttlekeswick@hotmail.com.*

Lá brea dhuit amach ar na sléibhte!
Agus cupán tae deas dhuit ag deire an lae.

Walk 1

Newlands Valley

Type of walk	A 'figure of eight' walk using the lake launch.
Distance	6 miles *(excluding distance travelled by launch)*
Total Feet of ascent	Negligible.
Suggested time	2^1/$_2$ hours.
Public transport	Derwentwater launch. See page 36 .

This is a walk from Keswick to Little Town in the Newlands valley which is a particularly pastoral looking valley surrounded by an array of graceful peaks which Coleridge often likened to giant tents. The way back involves using the lake launch. This adds novelty to the walk and, of course, makes it a little shorter. For devotees of the works of Beatrix Potter the walk will have an added interest. Little Town features in *The Tale of Mrs Tiggy-Winkle*.

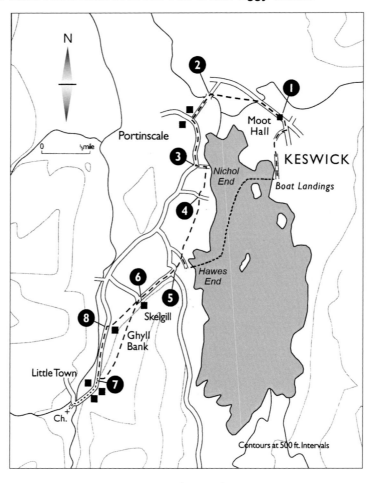

1 From the Moot Hall walk westwards down hill along Main Street to the bridge spanning the River Greta. Immediately after crossing the bridge turn left on to a trackway following the river and pass through the first gate on your right on to a broad pathway crossing two large fields to reach a roadway. Here turn left to reach a suspended footbridge spanning the River Derwent. (1 mile)

2 Cross over the bridge and continue straight ahead in to the village of Portinscale. On reaching a T junction turn left and continue on this road until you come to a driveway leading off to the left signposted as leading to Nichol End. (3/4 mile)

3 Follow the driveway to the lakeshore and then continue along a track to your right leading behind Nichol End Marine. This crosses over a surfaced driveway and then leads behind Fawe Park House and its gardens to another surfaced driveway. (1/2 mile)

4 Cross straight over the driveway and continue through a narrow gate on to an enclosed path clearly signposted on the gate as leading to Cat Bells. Initially the path leads to yet another driveway, leading to Hawes End. Again cross over this driveway on to a path directly opposite, to climb uphill slightly, a hundred yards or so, to reach a public road. (3/4 mile)

5 Follow the road uphill, across a cattle grid, to a sharp hairpin bend. Here you should bear right and continue on a road signposted as leading to Skelgill. (1/2 mile)

6 At the hamlet of Skelgill the road turns sharp right and leads downhill. Follow the road's descent but a few yards and on reaching an old water trough turn sharp left off the road on to a path leading immediately past the gable end of what used to be Skelgill Farm. This path leads to Little Town across a series of fields mostly following a line of hawthorn bushes. (1 mile)

(Little Town is the the turning point on this walk. It is, however, well worth progressing a little further to visit Newlands Church. To do so follow the road through the hamlet and on a further couple of hundred yards. After crossing a bridge spanning Newlands Beck the road curves right. At this point a gated road leads off to the left. Newlands Church is little more than a hundred yards along this road.)

7 Here turn right. A little more than half a mile along the road, after a sharp bend, is Ghyll Bank Farm. A few yards past Ghyll Bank on your right locate a small gate from which a signposted path leads back to Skelgill. (1/2 mile)

8 Follow this path to Skelgill and from there retrace your outward route as far as the driveway leading to Hawes End. Turn right. Within a hundred yards along this driveway veer off to the left on to a signposted path to "Hawes End Jetty". From the jetty board a lake launch to transport yourself to the Keswick Boat Landings. From this point proceed northwards to the centre of Keswick. (1 1/2 miles, *excluding the distance travelled by launch*)

Walk 2

Langstrath

Type of walk	Circular.
Distance	7¹/₂ miles.
Total Feet of ascent	500 feet.
Suggested time	3 hours.
Starting point	Rosthwaite car park next to village hall (NY 268 045).
Public transport	Keswick to Seatoller bus service. See page 36.

This walk is perhaps the best level walk in the Lake District for anyone with a strong aversion to tackling steep gradients but who yet still desires to see something of the wild nature of the Cumbrian fells. The name Langstrath simply means long valley, which it is: long, wild and empty of habitation.

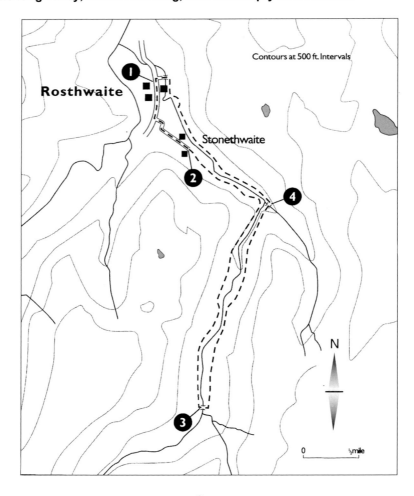

1   From Rosthwaite continue south along the valley's main road (the B5289) and take the first turn left along a road signposted as leading to Stonethwaite. (1 mile)

2   At the end of the hamlet of Stonethwaite, just past the Langstrath Hotel, the road continues as a trackway. Three quarters of a mile from Stonethwaite the track turns south into the valley of Langstrath. Just over a mile along the valley the trackway comes to a five bar gate. Once through this gate the track becomes a somewhat indistinct pathway crossing a broad flat grassy section of the the valley floor. The path becomes more evident after a few hundred yards on reaching rockier ground. Just before reaching the confluence of Stake Beck with Langstrath Beck the path comes to a sturdy footbridge spanning Langstrath Beck. ($2^{3/4}$ miles)

3   Cross over the footbridge and before climbing uphill bear left a few yards to avoid a soggy section of fellside. After climbing fifty feet or so you should come upon a distinct path. Here turn left and follow the path northwards along the eastern side of the valley to the confluence of Langstrath Beck and Greenup Gill, where you come to the Gordon Hallworth Bridge spanning Greenup Gill. (2 miles)

4   Cross over this bridge and pass through a gate on the other side onto a pathway. Here turn left. The path soon becomes a broad attractive trackway leading back to Rosthwaite. On reaching a surfaced access road turn left and follow the access road over a stone bridge back into Rosthwaite. ($1^{13/4}$ miles)

[N.B. *An excellent way of concluding this walk is to enjoy the tea and scones which are served daily in the Royal Oak Hotel in Rosthwaite between 3.45 and 5 p.m. all year round except for a few weeks in December and January.]*

The Gordon Hallworth Bridge

The footbridge used in this walk spanning Greenup Gill is dedicated to the memory of Gordon Hallworth who died at the age of 21 a short distance upstream from the bridge in January 1939. With a group of fellow students from Manchester University where he was studying physics he was on a winter walking trip to the Lake District. With two companions Gordon Hallworth had climbed Glaramara and Allen Crags and was returning to Rosthwaite via Langstrath. The group intended crossing Greenup Gill by way of a bridge which was seemingly situated where the Hallworth Bridge is today. Unfortunately they were unaware this bridge had been swept away some years earlier. Darkness had fallen and their torch malfunctioned. Unable to consult their map they were unaware of an alternative bridge they could have used. Tragically they thought they had no option but to ford Greenup Gill. Being in spate they were forced to follow the river upstream before they could do so. They met with great difficulties. The exertions needed to meet those difficulties proved too much for the young man whose memorial is the bridge we use today.

Walk 3   The Derwentwater Circuit

Type of walk	Circular.
Distance	9 miles.
Total feet of ascent	Imperceptible.
Suggested time	3 hours.

During, and after, heavy periods of rainfall the southern part of this walk is likely to be flooded. The walk then is only feasible if you wear waders!

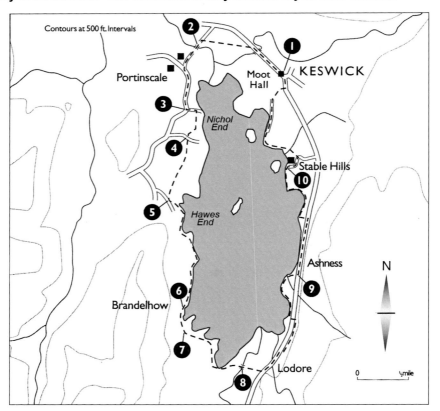

1 From the Moot Hall walk westwards downhill along Main Street to the bridge spanning the River Greta. After crossing the bridge turn immediately left onto a trackway following the river and pass through the first gate on your right on to a broad pathway crossing two large fields leading to another roadway. Here turn left to reach a suspended footbridge. (1 mile)

2 Cross over the bridge and continue straight ahead into Portinscale. On coming to a T junction turn left and continue along the road till you come to a driveway, on your left, signposted as leading to Nichol End. (1/2 mile)

10

3   Follow the driveway to the lake shore and then continue along a trackway to your right leading behind Nichol End Marine. This crosses over a surfaced driveway leading to Fawe Park House and then passes the gardens of the house and eventually reaches another surfaced driveway. (^{1}/$_2$ mile)

4   Cross over this driveway and continue through a small gate opposite on which is a small sign bearing the words: "Miles without Stiles". The pathway leading from the gate eventually comes to yet another driveway. Here turn left. The driveway immediately branches in two. Follow the right-hand branch. Within a hundred yards, on the left-hand side of the driveway, is the start of a signposted path to Hawes End Jetty. (^{3}/$_4$ mile)

5   Follow the path down to the jetty. Here, to your right leading southwards, begins a lake shore path. Veering a few yards from the lake the path soon links to a trackway. Here turn left. The trackway reduces to a path as it moves back to the lake shore. The path then stays very close to the lake shore all the way to the Brandelhow boat landing. (1^1/$_4$ miles)

6   From the landing stage keep to the water's edge along a very gravelly shoreline. On reaching a fence a wooden gate comes in to view. From the gate proceed towards the gap between the house and outer shed now directly ahead of you. Here commences the start of a trackway. The trackway almost immediately splits in two. Keep to the right branch leading to a slate cottage called the Warren. Directly opposite the cottage is the start of a distinct, broad pathway leading through woodland. (^{1}/$_4$ mile)

7   After a few hundred yards the path comes a stone wall Set in the wall, fifty yards from the lake shore, is a gateway. Beyond the gateway the path continues over very boggy ground by way of a series of duckboards. These duckboards not only make the route feasible they also make it very obvious as to where to proceed. The duckboards lead to a footbridge spanning the River Derwent. (^{3}/$_4$ mile)

8   From the bridge a broad path leads to the Borrowdale Road. Here turn left. Roughly a hundred yards past the Lodore Hotel on your right is the start of a path that parallels the road. Where this path rejoins the road, on the other side of the road, is the start of a shore line path. After proceeding around a delta of land projecting into the lake the path returns back to the road. (1^1/$_4$ miles)

9   From this point it is possible to keep to the lake shore though it is very rocky and none too easy to walk on. The road, therefore, despite the traffic, is perhaps preferable to walk along. Within a few hundred yards you will find there is roadside pathway. Where the space between the lake shore and road widens, and is filled by woodland, a boundary wall lines the left-hand side of the road. From a break in the wall, a path leads down to the lake shore. Here the lake shore path is much easier to walk on. Continue northwards along this path to Stable Hills. (1^1/$_4$ miles)

10   From Stable Hills follow, for a few hundred yards, the access trackway leading to the houses, and then branch left onto a path passing through a small gate next to a six bar gate. This path leads through a small belt of woodland emerging from which it continues along the lake shore, eventually reaching a surfaced roadway. Continue along the roadway back to Keswick. (1^1/$_4$ mile)

Latrigg 1203 feet

Type of walk	Circular.
Distance	6 miles.
Total Feet of ascent	1000 feet.
Suggested time	3 hours.

Latrigg is Keswick's own personal fell. Its close proximity and steep rising slopes make it an imposing presence. Yet in reality it is only a modest fell, little more than a third the height of its giant neighbour Skiddaw, and there is little that is dramatic about the fell itself. Its slopes are almost entirely smooth and unbroken by crags, steep as they are. The reward for climbing Latrigg is not in exploring the fell itself but the view from it. The same qualities that make it imposing to look at from Keswick, its proximity and steepness, make it a remarkable place from which to look down on the town. A half hour can easily go by whilst you pick out the places you might be familiar with. Lifting your eyes higher the view is of no less interest. From Latrigg on a clear day the full length of Borrowdale is visible, and at the valley's head England's loftiest mountains.

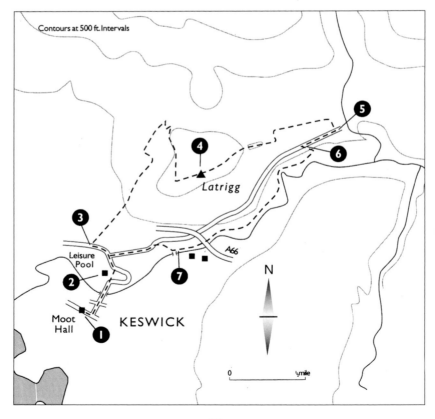

1   From the entrance of the Moot Hall walk between the Britannia Building Society and the baker's shop and turn first left into Station Street. Continue to the top of Station Street and across the main Penrith Road, where Station Street becomes Station Road, and to the top of Station Road to where the leisure pool is situated. ($^1/_2$ mile)

2   Walk round the leisure pool to the car park at the rear. At the exit from the car park, at a miniature roundabout, turn left along Brundholme Road which merges into Briar Rigg Road. A few hundred yards along this road on your right is the start of Spoony Green Lane, a trackway signposted as being a bridleway leading to Skiddaw. ($^1/_4$ mile)

3   The track crosses over the A66 and then ascends the western slopes of Latrigg. About a mile from the start of the track, after passing a wooden gate on your left giving access to a plantation of conifers, begin looking on your right for the start of a pathway signposted as leading to Latrigg Summit. The path turns acutely off to the right from the trackway and takes a graceful, partially zigzagged, course to the top of the fell. ($1^1/_2$ miles)

4   Follow the summit ridge north-eastwards to a six bar gate beyond which continue straight ahead along the ill-defined crest of the fell's north-eastern ridge. (Whilst there is not quite a path it is evident where people have trod.) Eventually the path reaches a wire fence and a line of spindly hawthorn bushes. Here turn left and follow the fence to a metal farm gate. From this gate a trackway continues to follow the tapering north-eastern ridge until it finally reaches a roadway. ($1^1/_4$ miles)

5   Here turn right. The road leads back to Keswick. There is, however, a mostly off road alternative way back to Keswick: a woodland path running at a level below that of the roadway. The start of this route begins fifty yards from the point where the road is enclosed on both sides by Brundholme wood. ($^1/_4$ mile)

6   Here leading acutely off to the left is the start of a trackway leading into the wood. The track soon makes a sharp right-hand turn. From this sharp turn a couple of hundred yards further begin looking for the start of a distinct path leading off to the right. (Ignore the green waymark which suggests you should keep to the track.)   This is a partially constructed path and takes an undulating course back to Keswick.   After passing under the impressive concrete bridge supporting the A66 the path approaches a much older stone bridge. (1 mile)

7   Do not cross the stone bridge but follow the trackway which crosses over it. The trackway proceeds around the isolated building that stands next to the bridge; briefly runs along the river's edge and then leads uphill to the Calvert Trust Riding Centre where it joins a roadway. Here turn left and follow the road back towards Keswick.   On reaching a road junction you will doubtless recognise this as the junction you passed at the beginning of the walk. Here turn left and retrace your earlier route back to Keswick. ($1^1/_4$ miles)

Keswick to Rosthwaite

Type of walk	Outward walk, return by the Borrowdale bus.
Distance	7 miles.
Total Feet of ascent	1500 feet.
Suggested time	4 hours.
Public transport	Seatoller to Keswick bus service. See page 36.

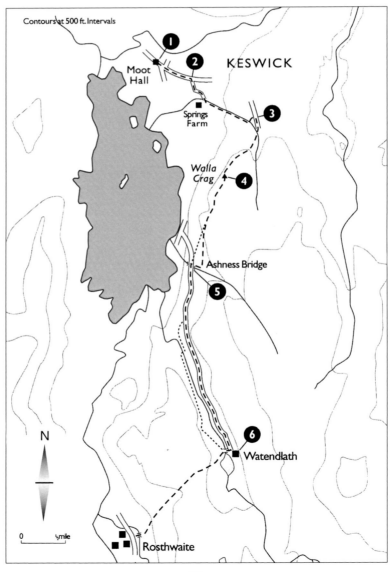

This is a very varied walk. It begins with an ascent of Walla Crag followed by a descent to Ashness Bridge on which there are some inspiring views of Borrowdale. From the bridge the route then continues along a secretive narrow valley to the sequestered tarn and hamlet of Watendlath. Finally, after a short ascent, there is pleasing descent to Rosthwaite with further impressive views of Borrowdale.

(An easier start to this walk, which excludes Walla Crag, is to follow the High Seat and Bleaberry Fell Walk described on pages 26 and 27 as far as Ashness Bridge, and then continue from directional note 5 below. This reduces the amount of climbing involved by six hundred feet.)

1   From the Moot Hall walk between the Britannia Building Society and the baker's shop into St. John's Street and past St. John's Church where it becomes the Ambleside Road. Just before the road begins to climb steeply uphill turn right into Springs Road. (3 furlongs)

2   Walk to the end of the road to Springs Farm. After crossing a small bridge at the entrance to the farm the route bears left past a stable block and then follows the course of Brockle Beck. Ignore the first footbridge spanning the beck but continue some four hundred yards further uphill to a second footbridge. Cross this bridge and continue up to a gateway giving access to a roadway. (1 mile)

3   Here turn right and walk to the end of the road where another footbridge crosses Brockle Beck. On the other side of the bridge is the start of a very distinct path which follows the line of a stone wall to the summit of Walla Crag. The summit cairn is situated a few yards behind the wall. ($^3/_4$ mile)

4   From the summit cairn continue southwards along a well worn path to a stile. Almost immediately after crossing the stile the path branches in two; take the left-hand branch which contours the fellside. Some two hundred yards from the summit of Walla Crag a path branches off to the left towards Bleaberry Fell. Ignore this path and keep to the broader path you are on which, after passing above Falcon Crag, descends to Barrow Beck which you then should follow down stream to Ashness Bridge. It is easy to miss this precise route and take instead a path which leads directly to Ashness Bridge. But in either case you should hopefully arrive at the same location. ($1^1/_4$ miles)

5   Follow the road which crosses Ashness Bridge uphill to the hamlet of Watendlath. *(Or alternatively, some three quarters of a mile from Ashness Bridge, where the road levels, branch right on to broad pathway which leads to a footbridge spanning Watendlath Beck giving access to a path which follows the course of the beck to the hamlet of Watendlath.)* (2 miles)

6   From the hamlet of Watendlath, beginning from the outflow of the tarn next to which the hamlet is situated, a very broad pathway leads uphill out of the valley. After a short climb the path descends into Borrowdale and the village of Rosthwaite. ($1^1/_2$ miles) *[For a suggestion as to refreshments in Rosthwaite see the* nota bene *on page 9]*

RETURN: From the walk's concluding objective - the Rosthwaite village bus shelter - board one of the frequent buses back to Keswick.

Keswick to Seatoller

Type of walk	Outward walk, return by the Borrowdale bus.
Distance	8 miles.
Total Feet of ascent	1200 feet.
Suggested time	4 hours.
Public transport	Seatoller to Keswick bus service. See page 36.

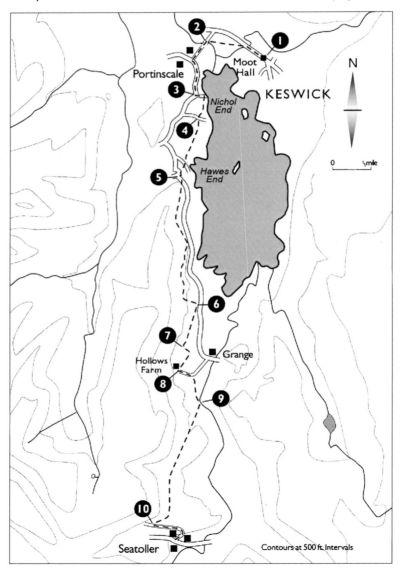

This is a walk to the head of Borrowdale mainly following a series of terraced pathways along the western side of the valley.

1   From the Moot Hall walk westwards downhill along Main Street to the bridge spanning the River Greta. After crossing the bridge turn immediately left onto a trackway following the river and pass through the first gate on your right on to a broad pathway which crosses two large fields and leads to another roadway. Here turn left to reach a suspended footbridge. (1 mile)

2   Cross over the bridge and continue straight ahead into Portinscale. On coming to a T junction turn left and continue along the road till you come to a driveway, on your left, signposted as leading to Nichol End. ($^{1}/_{2}$ mile)

3   Follow the driveway to the lake shore. Here continue on a trackway to your right leading behind Nichol End Marine which crosses the driveway to Fawe Park and eventually arrives at the surfaced driveway to Lingholm. ($^{1}/_{2}$ mile)

4   Cross over this driveway to a gateway which gives access to an enclosed pathway signposted as leading to Cat Bells. The path leads eventually to another driveway. Cross this driveway on to a path directly opposite which climbs uphill and within a hundred yards or so joins a public road. ($^{3}/_{4}$ mile)

5   Follow the road uphill to a cattle grid. Pass through a kissing gate to the left of the grid and continue on a short steep path that links up with the road again. At this point on the other side of the road is the start of a trackway which goes on to traverse the eastern slopes of Cat Bells. At one point, the site of an old quarry, the trackway briefly rejoins the road, but within the space of a few yards it leads off to the right again. On reaching a stone wall the track narrows; as the wall has been built over much of the trackway! After passing the wall the track broadens out again and leads downhill to a five bar gate. (1$^{3}/_{4}$ miles)

6   From the gate leading off to the right, initially following a wire fence, is a pathway signposted as leading to Hollows Farm. The path takes an undulating course and eventually reaches a small water treatment plant. ($^{3}/_{4}$ mile)

7   Here turn left and follow the line of the wall enclosing the nearby woodland downhill to join up with a trackway where it forms a sharp hairpin bend. Follow the lower part of this trackway to Hollows Farm. ($^{1}/_{4}$ mile)

8   Pass through the farmyard and continue on the farm's access road. Two hundred yards from the farm a trackway bears off to the right which eventually reaches the banks of the River Derwent where it makes a wide curve. ($^{1}/_{4}$ mile)

9   From the corner of this curve a trackway, signposted as leading to Honister and Seatoller, strikes uphill following Broadslack Gill. After a climb of roughly five hundred feet the track levels. Roughly a hundred yards along this level section, marked with a large cairn and a blue waymark, a path branches off to the left. This path contours the fellside, mostly following the line of a stone wall, and eventually joins the old toll road to Honister Pass. (1$^{1}/_{2}$ miles)

10   Turn left and follow the track down to Seatoller car park. ($^{1}/_{2}$ mile)

RETURN to Keswick by bus. A bus shelter is located at the exit to the car park.

Castlerigg Stone Circle
& St. John's in the Vale

Type of walk	Circular
	(or a linear walk to point 5: returning by bus)
Distance	11 miles *(4 miles linear)*
Total feet of ascent	900 feet.
Suggested time	5 hours *(2 hours linear)*

St. John's in the Vale is one of Lakeland's least frequented valleys but its attractiveness far from warrants this neglect. This walk can be made a linear walk by walking to the commencement of directional note 5 and then using the Windermere to Keswick bus service to return to Keswick. See page 36.

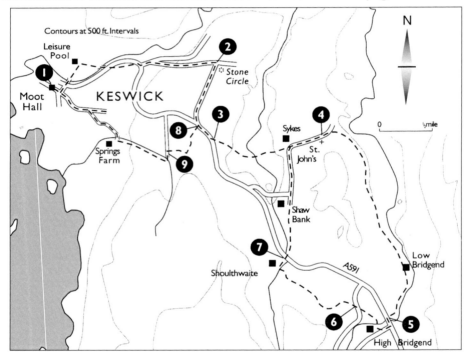

1   From the Moot Hall walk past Keswick Lodge and turn left in to Station Street which, continuing as Station Road, after passing the cenotaph, leads to Keswick's Leisure Pool. From the pool walk eastwards along the old railway line which is now a bridleway. Immediately after passing under a road bridge locate a flight of steps to your left. Ascend these steps to the main road. Here turn left and continue uphill. The road soon forks. Bear left on to the branch leading to Penrith. Within forty yards a minor road leads off to the right signposted as leading to Castlerigg Stone Circle. (1¹/₂ miles)

2 A few yards before reaching the stone circle a narrow road leads off to the right: Castle Lane. Follow this lane to its junction with the A591. Cross over the road on to a roadside footpath on the other side and walk downhill. Twenty yards after passing the entrance to Low Nest Farm cross back over the road to a stone stile - the start of a path signposted as leading to St. John's in the Vale. (³/4 mile)

3 Walk straight across the first field to another stone stile, then along the edge of a second field to a metal gate on to a trackway. Where the track crosses over some wooden sleepers the path to St. John's goes off to the left towards a small gate leading to a footbridge. From the footbridge the path crosses the next two fields to a kissing gate and then crosses the next field to a second kissing gate which gives access to a rough surfaced roadway. Follow this road uphill to St. John's in the Vale church. (1 mile)

4 Continue downhill from the church. Within less than a hundred yards pass through a gate on your right on to a path indicated as being a bridleway. A mile from the church, just before reaching a small barn, the bridleway appears to branch in two, the left branch leading across the valley floor to a stone bridge. Take the right-hand branch which leads behind the barn and on past Low Bridgend Farm to eventually reach the A591. *[Nearby a bus shelter provides the option of returning to Keswick by bus should you wish.]* (2¹/4 miles)

5 Here turn left and take the first turn right to High Bridgend Farm. Pass through the farmyard and sheep pens to a footbridge spanning St. John's Beck. Cross the bridge and follow a waymarked path to a group of barns. Pass between the barns and follow a trackway that leads from the barns to a surfaced road. Here turn right. Within twenty yards pass through the first gate on your left on to a broad trackway. (¹/2 mile)

6 Within a couple of hundred yards the trackway forks. Take the left-hand branch. Where this trackway begins to climb notice a grassier trackway to the right. This trackway leads to Shoulthwaite Farm. From the farm follow the farm's access road back to the main A591. (1 mile)

7 Cross straight over the road to a small stile. The stile gives access to a small field on the other side of which is another stile which gives access to an old section of the main road. From this stile diagonally opposite, on the other side of the road, is the start of a signposted bridleway. The bridleway leads to Shaw Bank where it becomes a narrow surfaced road. Follow this road to the entrance to Sykes Farm where you rejoin your outward route. Retrace your outward route to the junction of Castle Lane with the main A591. (2 miles)

8 On the left-hand side of the A591, opposite the start of Castle Lane, a gateway gives access to a signposted path to Keswick. Continue on this path which follows the right-hand side of three successive fields, then turns sharply right, crosses two further fields and eventually comes to a roadway. (¹/2 mile)

9 Here turn left. Within a few yards on the right is a kissing gate giving access to a footpath leading to a footbridge. From the bridge the path follows the course of the stream you have just crossed downhill to Springs Farm situated at the end of Springs Road. Follow Springs Road to its junction with the Ambleside Road. Here turn left to reach the centre of Keswick. (1¹/2 miles)

Walk 8

Lord's Seat 1813 ft.
& Barf 1536 ft.

Type of walk	Circular.
Distance	4½ miles.
Total Feet of ascent	1000 feet.
Suggested time	2½ hours.
Starting point	Whinlatter Visitors' Centre (NY 207 245).
Public transport	Honister Rambler bus service. See page 36.

This walk has the advantage of starting from 1000 feet. Much of it, however, is through thick afforestation and along dull forestry roads, but the views from Lord's Seat make it all worthwhile. From Lord's Seat on a good day can be seen Scotland, the Irish Sea, the Isle of Man and a good half of the Lakeland fells.

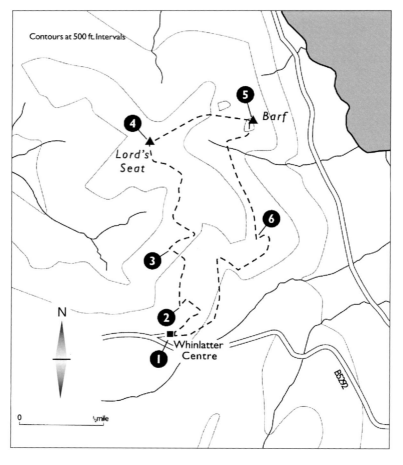

1   Begin by following the path which starts from the rear of the Whinlatter Centre Tearoom signposted with the word: "Trails". Follow the path that is waymarked with posts that have red, blue and green bands. After passing through a children's play area the path comes to a cleared viewpoint area. Leading steeply uphill from this viewpoint area, through the conifers, is a path waymarked with a post that just has a green band. This leads to a forest road. On reaching the forest road turn left. The forest road within a matter of yards branches in three. (1/4 mile)

2   Take the right-hand main branch. Where the road levels another forest road branches off to the right passing a post bearing the number "3". (1/2 mile)

3   Follow the right-hand branch. This road follows a winding course. Where it splits in two bear left. The track gradually reduces to a footpath which links on to a path following the crest of the ridge linking Seat How to Lord's Seat, at which point is a post bearing the number "5". Here turn left and follow the crest path to the top of Lord's Seat. (3/4 mile)

4   From the top of Lord's Seat a distinct path leads east on to Barf. (3/4 mile)

5   From the top of Barf a path descends to Beckstone Gill, crossing which it comes to a forestry fence. Beyond this fence the path links on to a forestry track. The track leads uphill slightly and joins a much broader forestry road. Follow the forestry road downhill to where it joins another forestry road and turn left. (1 mile)

6   This new forestry road almost immediately forms a sharp hairpin bend which curves right and leads downhill. Where it comes to a junction with another forest road turn right. This road leads back to the Whinlatter Centre. (1 1/4 miles)

A Dubious Lakeland "Legend"

On the steep eastern slopes of Barf is a large white painted rock known as Bishop Rock. A number of sources have it that in 1783 the newly appointed bishop of Derry was staying at the Swan Hotel, at the foot of Barf, whilst on his way to Ireland. After becoming inebriated with the inn's hospitality he wagered he could ride his horse to the summit of Barf. Both the bishop and his steed were killed in the attempt. Hence the rock received its name and has been painted white ever since to commemorate the event. No guide book written in the nineteenth century, however, mentions this astonishing tale. This is hardly surprising as in 1783 the then Catholic bishop of Derry, Philip McDevitt, had another fourteen years to live, and the Protestant bishop, Frederick Augustus Hervey, who was also the fourth Earl of Bristol, had yet another twenty years to live. The Protestant bishop died in Italy on the road to Albano, "in the outhouse of a peasant who could not admit a heretic prelate into his cottage". The legend behind Bishop Rock, therefore, seems likely to have been concocted by a past proprietor of the Swan Inn.

Walk 9

Brund Fell 1363 ft.
& King's How 1250 ft.

Type of walk	Circular.
Distance	5¹/₂ miles.
Total Feet of ascent	1500 feet.
Suggested time	3¹/₂ hours.
Starting point	Rosthwaite car park next to village hall (NY 268 045).
Public transport	Keswick to Seatoller bus. See page 36.

This is a short undulating circular walk over terrain that is decidedly different from the rest of the Lake District. Around Dock Tarn the surface of the fell is covered with an unusual mixture of broken rock and heather, whilst between Brund Fell and King's How individual knolls of crag form several miniature peaks. If anywhere in the Lake District can be said to attain the surreal it is here. This is a walk then with a wide variety of interest, well worth undertaking the steep initial climb it requires.

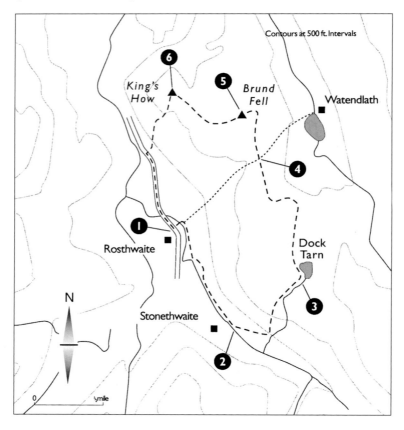

22

1   From the Rosthwaite bus shelter walk a few yards north towards Keswick and take the first turn right onto a narrow surfaced road.   Immediately after crossing a stone bridge turn sharp right and follow a bridleway which initially follows the side of the river you have just crossed. Where this bridleway turns sharp right into Stonethwaite keep progressing straight ahead through a five bar gate along a bridleway signposted as leading to Grasmere. Immediately after passing through a second five bar gate a grassy path leads uphill to the left. (1 mile)

2   This becomes a very steep but well pitched path ascending through an oak wood. Emerging from which the gradient soon eases and the path continues through an unusual terrain of broken rock and heather to Dock Tarn. (3/4 mile)

    [Lest it never be recorded elsewhere let it be recorded here that the path ascending to Dock Tarn is an example of the fine work undertaken by Ray McHaffie and the National Trust workers he supervised. For over twenty years Ray McHaffie was engaged in constructing footpaths for the National Trust until he retired in 2001. Nearly every walker in the Borrowdale area today is a beneficiary of his past labours.]

3   From Dock Tarn continue along the path following the western side of the tarn. A few hundred yards after leaving the tarn the path begins descending to Watendlath. Passing through a gateway the path begins to follow a series of blue topped wooden posts. Half a mile from Watendlath these posts then follow another path veering off sharply to the left towards a wire fence. (Or at least the most obvious set of posts do, confusingly another set continues following the path down to Watendlath.) The posts lead to a five bar gate and kissing gate set in the wire fence. Here the posts end, but the path leading from the gates is clear enough and leads to a broad pathway which is the Watendlath to Rosthwaite bridleway. (1 1/4 miles)

4   Cross straight over this bridleway and follow the path which follows the uphill course of the wall directly ahead of you. A few hundred yards along this wall is a wooden stile. Ignore this stile and keep climbing uphill. Nearing the top of the fell a second stile is reached. Cross over this stile and continue along the path on the other side to the top of Brund Fell. (1/2 mile)

5   The path slightly bypasses the summit of Brund Fell and continues straight ahead. This is a well defined path that descends downhill, eventually reaching a wire fence at the foot of King's How. Cross over the fence and follow the steep worn path directly ahead to the top of King's How. (1/2 mile)

6   From the top of King's How a path descends southwards towards Rosthwaite. This path soon splits in two. Bear right. From here the path becomes more defined twisting through birches and occasional yews. Reaching a ruined wall the path again splits in two. Follow the left-hand path which passes through the wall. This is a thin but discernible path until it reaches a point a couple of hundred feet above the valley road where it seems to split in three! Take the left branch.   This soon links up with a more defined path leading to the roadway. On reaching the road turn left and follow it back to Rosthwaite. (1 1/4 miles)

Walk 10

Cat Bells 1481 ft.
& High Spy 2143 ft.

Type of walk   A linear walk between two points of public transport.
Distance   6¹/₂ miles.
Total Feet of ascent 2200 feet.
Suggested time   4¹/₂ hours.
Public transport   Lake launch and the Borrowdale bus. See page 36.

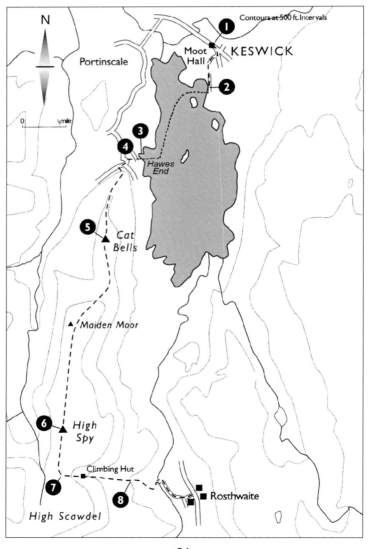

Though Cat Bells is one of Lakeland's smaller peaks its distinctive shape makes it a popular summit with walkers. By including Maiden Moor and High Spy the ascent of Cat Bells can be made part of a more satisfying ridge walk concluding with a steep, but rewarding, descent into Borrowdale.

(An alternative start to this walk which avoids using the lake launch is to follow the Newlands valley walk on pages 6&7 as far as directional note 5 and then continue from directional note 4 below. This adds two and a quarter miles to the walk.)

1   From the Moot Hall walk betwixt the Old Keswickian and the Dog and Gun in to Lake Road. At Fisher's turn right in to the continuation of Lake Road now semi-pedestrianised. From the road's cul-de-sac proceed through an underpass and then along a broad pathway running along the side of Hope Park miniature golf course and Crow Park to the Derwentwater Keswick boat landings. ($^1/_2$ mile)

2   Journey to Hawes End using the lake launch. See page 36.

3   From the Hawes End landing walk uphill along a broad pathway to a surfaced driveway. Here turn right. Within a hundred yards veer left on to a signposted path which within two hundred yards joins a public road. ($^1/_4$ mile)

4   Continue uphill over a cattlegrid for two hundred yards to a sharp hairpin bend where there is also a road junction. From the corner of the junction is the start of an obvious pathway that leads to the summit of Cat Bells. (1 mile)

5   From the summit of Cat Bells continue south, descending some two hundred and fifty feet to begin with, and then ascend a very distinct path which leads on to Maiden Moor and then on to the summit of High Spy. ($2^1/_2$ miles)

6   From the summit of High Spy follow a well worn path descending southwards. Roughly one hundred feet above the point where the path joins a swift flowing beck running through an incised gully, a very indistinct grassy path veers off to the left towards the gap between High Spy and High Scawdel. The start of the path is marked by a single cairn. The ground here is very flat and boggy and the path hardly exists after a hundred yards or so. Head for a prominent cairn on a small outcrop, just to the right of the centre of the gap. ($^3/_4$ mile)

7   Immediately beyond the cairn is a very simple stile athwart a wire fence giving access to a distinct path that descends through some former quarry workings. After roughly four hundred feet of descent a thinner more level path veers off to the right towards a group of old quarry buildings, one of which is now a climbing hut. From the hut a grassy path leads downhill. As you near a stone wall contouring the fellside, roughly five hundred feet below the climbing hut, head for a five bar gate that is set in the wall slightly to your left. ($^3/_4$ mile)

8   From the gate a grassy track leads directly downhill into the valley eventually arriving at a stile in the bottom corner of the field you enter. From the stile the path follows the final section of Tongue Gill to its confluence with the River Derwent. Follow the River Derwent down stream a few score yards to New Bridge. Cross New Bridge and follow the trackway which leads from it directly to Rosthwaite. *(See the* nota bene *on page 9 regarding sustenance.)* (1 mile)

RETURN to Keswick by bus - a bus shelter is located in the village.

Walk 11

High Seat 1996 ft.
& Bleaberry Fell 1932 ft.

Type of walk	Circular.
Distance	9¼ miles.
Total Feet of ascent	2000 feet.
Suggested time	5 hours.

These two fell tops lying between Thirlmere and Derwentwater unfortunately have the consistency of an extremely well soaked sponge. This walk then is best done during a period of very dry weather or, better still, during a period of very hard frost.

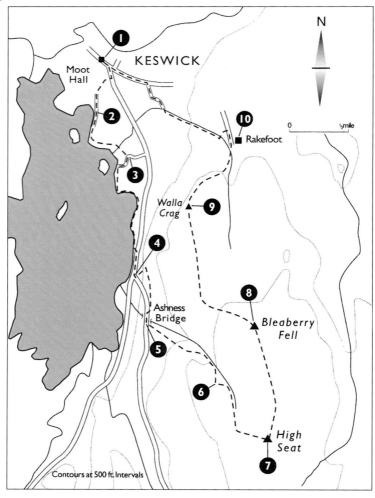

1   From the Moot Hall walk betwixt the Old Keswickian and the Dog and Gun in to Lake Road. At Fisher's turn right in to what is the continuation of Lake Road now semi-pedestrianised. From the road's cul-de-sac proceed through an underpass and then along a broad pathway running along the side of Hope Park, miniature golf course and Crow Park, to the lake shore. (^{1}/$_2$ mile)

2   Continue to the end of the road running next to the lake. Where it terminates it continues as a broad pathway. After a hundred yards this pathway branches in two. Take the left-hand branch. The path passes round the lake shore and then through woodland where it joins a trackway. (^{1}/$_2$ mile)

3   Turn right. After crossing a cattle grid branch left off the trackway on to a signposted pathway which follows the shore line of the lake. After three quarters of a mile it is necessary to leave the lake shore and scramble up to the Borrowdale Road. Continue along the road a futher four hundred yards or so to the start of the Watendlath Road. (1^1/$_4$ miles)

4   Continue uphill along the Watendlath Road. A hundred yards after crossing the cattle grid locate the start of a path leading sharply off to the left. After a short climb the path comes to a large cairn. Here turn right and follow a path signposted as leading to Ashness Bridge. (^{3}/$_4$ mile)

5   Continue on the road which crosses over the bridge. Sixty yards from the bridge, follow a signposted path leading off to the left which initially follows the course of a stone wall. After a steep climb the path comes to follow Ashness Gill very closely. At this point a path veers sharply uphill to the right. Ignore this path and keep following the stream. After a short distance this path too veers to the right from the beck. After a few hundred feet more level terrain is reached and the path intersects with another path. (^{3}/$_4$ mile)

6   At this intersection, if conditions are clear, High Seat is now visible. Turn left and follow the path heading for the top. The ground soon becomes very boggy and for all practical purposes the path disappears. At this point though you should now be following a very dilapidated wall. Continue to follow the wall which often provides the firmest footing. On reaching firmer ground, with the summit of High Seat now almost directly on your left, the path heads away from the wall directly for the top of High Seat. (1 mile)

7   From the summit of High Seat walk northwards along the ridge connecting it to Bleaberry Fell. initially following the remains of a metal fence. This path is more discernible but still very boggy. (1 mile)

8   From the summit of Bleaberry a path descends north-westwards over a 1000 feet where it links with a path leading northwards on to Walla Crag. (1^1/$_4$ miles)

9   From the summit of Walla Crag continue north-eastwards along a path descending to Rakefoot Farm. (^{3}/$_4$ mile)

10 Continue roughly 250 yards along the road leading to the farm to a kissing gate on the left-hand side of the road. The gate gives access to a path leading to a footbridge. From the bridge the path continues along the stream the bridge spans to Springs Farm. Follow the road which leads to the farm to a road junction. Here turn left to return to the centre of Keswick. (1^1/$_2$ miles)

Walk 12

Robinson 2417 ft.
& Dale Head 2473 ft.

Type of walk	A linear walk between two points of public transport.
Distance	7$^1/_2$ miles.
Total Feet of ascent	3000 feet.
Suggested time	5$^1/_2$ hours.
Starting point	Buttermere (NY 176 169).
Return point	Brandlelhow Boat Landing (NY 252 198).
Public transport	The Honister Rambler bus and lake launch. See page 36.

Within an hour of commencing the walk you should reach the shoulder of High Snockrigg - a more appealing top than its name suggests. The walk then undulates over Robinson, Dale Head, High Spy and Maiden Moor, providing splendid views of the valleys of Newlands, Buttermere and Borrowdale. The pleasing bonus at the end of the walk is the journey by launch across Derwentwater back to Keswick. On a long summer's evening it provides a wonderful conclusion to a day's walking on the fells. Brandelhow pier is also such a serene place if one has to wait there for a launch it becomes a pleasure.

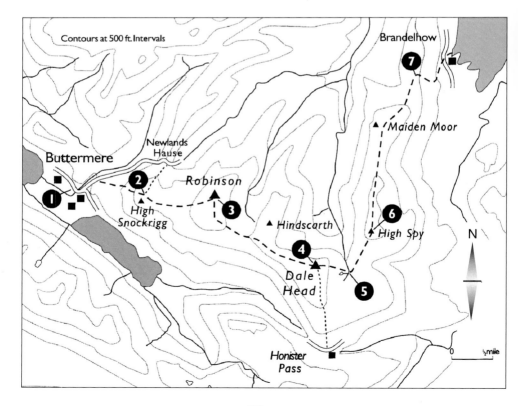

The start of this walk can be obtained by using the Honister Rambler bus service from Keswick to Buttermere. (See page 36).

1   Starting from the Bridge Hotel in Buttermere turn right and follow the road uphill past the former village school. Further on, after passing Buttermere Church, branch left on to the road signposted as leading to Keswick. A few hundred yards along this road, where it swings left, on the right hand side of the road a small wooden signpost indicates the start of a pathway striking boldly uphill. After a relentless climb of fourteen hundred feet the path comes to the shoulder of High Snockrigg and a flattish area of fell-land known as Buttermere Moss. (1 mile)

2   The path continues across Buttermere Moss as a thin trail and almost imperceptibly branches in two, each branch ascends to the top of Robinson: the right-hand branch, though, is probably the better of the two. Given adequate visibility the line of each path is fairly discernible at a distance if not always perceptible underfoot. (1 mile)

    [Before embarking on this ascent it is well worth making a slight diversion to the actual summit of High Snockrigg from which point some exceptional views of Buttermere are obtainable.]

3   From the top of Robinson head south along the summit ridge to a wire fence. Here turn left and follow the path initially following the line of this fence along an undulating ridge, across the shoulder of Hindscarth, and on to the summit of Dale Head. (1^3/$_4$ miles)

4   From the top of Dale Head continue eastwards along the edge of the fell. There soon follows a steep descent, much of it pitched, to the northern side of Dale Head Tarn. (1/2 mile)

5   The path continues round the northern edge of Dale Head Tarn and down to a deeply incised beck. Crossing over the beck the path turns northwards and climbs to the summit of High Spy. (3/4 mile)

6   From the top of High Spy the path continues northwards across Maiden Moor and then descends to the col between Maiden Moor and Cat Bells. (2 miles).

7   From this col a path descends down to the right, to the Grange to Portinscale road. About one hundred feet above a group of conifer trees surrounding a group of large houses, follow a distinct narrow path veering off to the left from the main path. This soon links up with a much broader pathway which you should follow northwards to where it meets the Grange to Portinscale road. Walk ten yards northwards along the road to a short flight of steps leading off to the right giving access to a rough pathway leading down to the lake shore. Follow the lake shore northwards a hundred yards or so to the Brandelhow landing stage. (1 mile)

RETURN to Keswick using the lake launch, or alternatively use the Honister Rambler service which uses the Grange to Portinscale road, or use the Honister Rambler to return to Buttermere. (See page 36).

Walk 13   # Blencathra 2847 ft.

Type of walk	Linear walk, outward journey by bus.
Distance	7¹/2 miles.
Total Feet of ascent	2400 feet.
Suggested time	5 hours.
Starting point	White Horse Inn, Scales. (NY 343 269).
Public transport	Keswick to Penrith bus services. See page 36.

Blencathra appears to be a mountain with no secrets. It rises boldly above the village of Threlkeld seemingly showing all its features. It does have one secret however: Scales Tarn. This walk reaches the summit via this hidden tarn: by far the most dramatic approach to the summit. I have not, however, included the route across Sharp Edge which overlooks the tarn, for although popular and usually quite negotiable it can be hazardous and tragedies have occurred on it. Once the summit is attained the route back to Keswick is quite easy: along the summit ridge and then down the eastern slope of Blencathra, concluding with a walk through the wooded slopes of Latrigg. Or, alternatively one can enjoy a pint in Threlkeld and then get a bus!

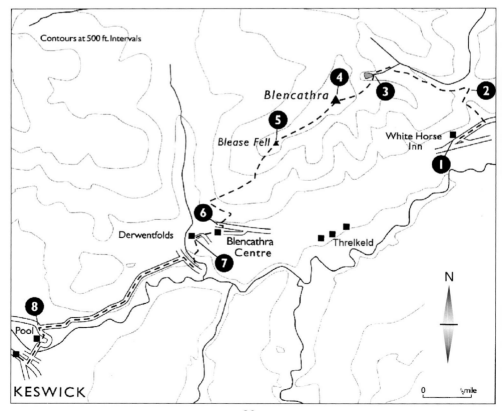

1   Beginning from the White Horse Inn turn left at the gable end of the building on to a minor road signposted as leading to Southerfell. Follow the road for just over a quarter of a mile to a signposted path leading off to the left in to Mousthwaite Comb, initially following a line of straggly hawthorn bushes. The path first climbs straight uphill and then takes a diagonal line of ascent to the top of the corrie. (1 mile)

2   From the top of Mousthwaite Comb the path continues to your left, westwards, along the ridge. After about a hundred yards the path veers off to the right and contours along the side of Scales Fell towards Sharp Edge eventually reaching a swift flowing beck which it follows upstream to Scales Tarn. ($1^{1}/_{4}$ miles)

3   From the outflow of the tarn, facing the tarn, follow the path climbing the fellside up to your left. This is not a distinct path and can be easily lost. If so, simply keep climbing uphill. On gaining the ridge a quite obvious path is to be found which leads to the summit. ($^{1}/_{2}$ mile)

4   From the summit follow the summit ridge south-westwards to the top of Blease Fell, the western shoulder of Blencathra. ($^{3}/_{4}$ mile)

5   From the top of Blease Fell continue to head in a south-westerly direction. Within a short distance a well worn, and well cairned path, becomes evident. As you descend this path try to discern a few hundred feet below two grassy pathways, one leading towards Threlkeld village, the other towards Keswick. After a particularly steep section the path becomes distinctly less worn. This is where the two paths meet. The path branching off to the right, towards Keswick, however, is so indistinct it can easily be missed. After following it a few yards, however, it becomes more discernible. Almost imperceptibly it merges in to a constructed pathway that turns towards Threlkeld. At about the 1200 foot contour another constructed pathway, leading to a small abandoned quarry on your left, cuts across this path. Here turn right and follow the quarry track down to a trackway running above the Blencathra Centre. ($1^{1}/_{4}$ miles)

6   Here turn left and walk sixty yards along the trackway to a cattle grid. Pass through the kissing gate to the right of the grid on to a path leading down to the driveway running through the centre. On reaching the driveway turn right. At the end of the driveway is the start of a clearly signposted path to Keswick, leading firstly to a surfaced access road to Derwentfolds Farm. ($^{1}/_{4}$ mile)

7   At the gable end of the Derwentfolds Farm is the start of a signposted path to Keswick leading to a footbridge spanning Glenderaterra Beck, from which there is a short steep climb up to a rough surfaced roadway. Here turn right and follow the road uphill. After turning left the road becomes better surfaced. After two miles it links to another road. ($2^{1}/_{4}$ miles)
    [For an alternative mainly off road route back to Keswick refer to directional notes 5 to 7 on page 13]

8   Here turn left to reach, within a few hundred yards, a small roundabout. Here turn right in to the Keswick Leisure Pool car park. Walk through the car park on to Station Road which leads directly to the centre of Keswick. ($^{1}/_{2}$ mile)

Walk 14

Glaramara 2560 ft.
& Allen Crags 2572 ft.

Type of walk	Circular.
Distance	8 miles.
Total Feet of ascent	2600 feet.
Suggested time	5¹/₂ hours.
Starting point	Seatoller car park (NY 245 138).
Public transport	Keswick to Seatoller bus service. See page 36.

For anyone who has never climbed a Lakeland summit Glaramara is a good fell to begin with. The ascent is fairly easy yet it still gives the walker a good appreciation of what the Cumbrian fells are like.

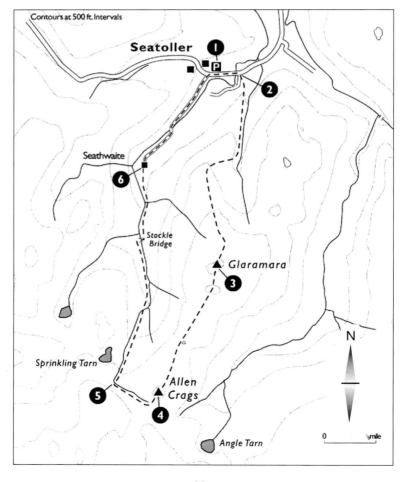

1   From Seatoller car park walk eastwards along the main road to Keswick for a quarter of a mile to Mountain View, a prominent terrace of cottages. Opposite Mountain View is a farm access road leading to Thorneythwaite Farm. Follow the access road some eighty yards till you come to a tall wooden stile on your left. (3 furlongs)

2   The stile gives access to a path which broadly follows the line of the ridge ahead of you to the summit of Glaramara. Half a mile from the stile the path comes to a kissing gate. Roughly two hundred and fifty yards further from the gate a path branches off to the left. Ignore this path and keep to the more prominent path climbing uphill. Near the summit of Glaramara there is a scramble of about a hundred feet. This is not difficult, but can be avoided if necessary by taking a wide curving course of ascent to the right. (2 miles)

3   From the summit of Glaramara continue south-westwards following a ridge path linking Glaramara to Allen Crags. The route is very undulating and quite rocky in places and passes a number of attractive pools and small tarns on the way. It is therefore a pleasing traverse but also requires more effort than the mileage alone suggests. ($1^{1}/_{2}$ miles)

4   Descend south-westwards off Allen Crags. At the foot of a short descent a cairn marks the intersection of the path you are following with a path running from Angle Tarn to Sprinkling Tarn. Here turn right and follow the path towards Sprinkling Tarn. The path soon parallels a deep gully. Half a mile from Allen Crags note a distinct piece of pitched path descending down to the beck running through the gully. ($^{1}/_{2}$ mile)

5   Descend to the beck and cross over it to follow the path leading out of the gully on the other side. This path continues northwards following the course of Ruddy Gill. Within a hundred yards or so it commences making a long descent eventually reaching Stockley Bridge. Cross over Stockley Bridge and continue along the trackway leading from it to Seathwaite Farm. ($2^{1}/_{4}$ miles)

6   Follow the road from Seathwaite back to Seatoller. ($1^{1}/_{4}$ miles)

[Sustenance in Seatoller can be obtained at "The Yew Tree", a fully licensed cafe - open seasonally. Other all year round options are to be found in Rosthwaite.]

Seathwaite's Unenviable Record

It is sometimes stated that Seathwaite is the wettest place in England, if not in Britain. Both statements are incorrect. It is the wettest *inhabited* place in England. The average annual rainfall is a little over 130 inches - more than twice the amount Keswick receives. Rain falls on Seathwaite nearly two days out of three. The farmyard in Seathwaite as well as receiving more raindrops than any other farmyard in England perhaps also receives more footfalls as well, as it is perhaps the most popular starting point for walks on the high fells in the Lake District.

Walk 15

Skiddaw 3054 ft.

Type of walk	A linear walk, outward journey by bus return on foot.
Distance	8 miles.
Total Feet of ascent	2900 feet.
Suggested time	6 hours.
Starting point	High Side Farm. (NY 235 305).
Public transport	For information on bus services between Keswick and High Side Farm See page 36

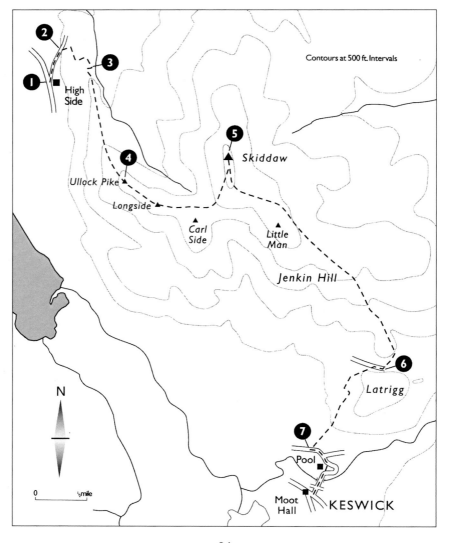

Contours at 500 ft. Intervals

High Side

Skiddaw

Ullock Pike

Longside

Carl Side

Little Man

Jenkin Hill

Latrigg

Pool

Moot Hall

KESWICK

N

0   ½ mile

This walk over Skiddaw undoubtedly provides the most interesting way to the summit. Though a popular mountain because of its height the mountain has little drama except on this particular route.

1   From High Side Farm continue along the minor road signposted as leading to Orthwaite to the start of a gated trackway on your right, just after passing a small lay-by. ($1/2$ mile)

2   Almost immediately after passing through the gate the trackway bifurcates. The official right of way is the left-hand track which crosses a beck and then follows a line of spindly hawthorn bushes. Follow the line of these bushes. Before they terminate you should be able to see a six bar gate in the wall away to your left, a hundred yards or so higher up the fell. Pass through this gate and walk on to the next gate a hundred yards ahead. After passing through this second gate follow the rutted trackway you come to by walking a few yards directly ahead.   The trackway curves southwards and comes to another gate. ($1/2$ mile)

3   After passing through this third gate (counting from the hawthorn bushes) turn immediately right and continue along the side of the wall which climbs uphill from the gate.   Where the wall reaches its highest point a very indistinct grassy path veers off to the left, diagonally tacking the slope of the ridge you have just reached the crest of.   In fact there are two parallel paths which quickly merge. The path becomes more evident the further you progress along it.   Within a short distance the path is joined by a path ascending from the Ravenstone Hotel.   The path is now quite distinct and there should be no problem following it to the summit of Ullock Pike. ($1 1/4$ miles)

4   From the top of Ullock Pike follow the ridge on to Longside. From Longside the path descends slightly and skirts round the the dome shaped summit of Carl Side to a shallow col between Carl Side and Skiddaw. From the col a diagonal path climbs up to the left to the summit of Skiddaw. ($1 1/2$ miles)

5   From the summit walk south to the end of the summit ridge where there is a good view overlooking Keswick. Here the path swings left. This is known as the 'tourist path' which you should have no problem following.   After descending five hundred feet the path traverses around Little Man and then commences a long descent of Jenkin Hill. At the 1100 foot contour the path reaches a level section and passes through a kissing gate and then progresses between two parallel fences to the terminus of a minor road. (3 miles)

6   Turn right. Follow the road sixty yards and pass through the first kissing gate on your left on to a signposted bridleway.   This trackway descends the western slopes of Latrigg and after crossing over the A66 joins Briar Rigg Road on the outskirts of Keswick. ($1 1/2$ miles)

7   Here turn left. Within a few hundred yards the road comes to a roundabout. Here turn right in to the Keswick Leisure Pool car park. Walk through the car park on to Station Road which leads directly to the centre of Keswick. ($1/2$ mile)

PUBLIC TRANSPORT

Buses

From Easter to October, buses in the Lake District carry stocks of a comprehensive timetable guide called "the Cumbria & Lakesrider" that covers all the bus services a visitor to Lakeland is likely to want to know about. Copies of this guide can also be obtained from Keswick's Tourist Information Centre in the Moot Hall in the centre of Keswick: telephone 72645. A similar guide, "Cumbria Rider", is produced for the winter months and is obtainable from the same sources.

The bus services used in this guide are as follows:-

For walks: 2, 5, 6, 9,10, and 14
Service 78 - Keswick to Seatoller: The Borrowdale Bus

For walk 7
Service 555/556 - High Bridgend to Keswick

For walks 8 and 12
Service 77/77A (seasonal) - The Honister Rambler
Keswick to Whinlatter and Buttermere

For walk 13
Services X5 and 73A (seasonal) - Keswick to the White Horse Inn
[NB. in 2012 Alba Travel operated a seasonal service from Keswick to Patterdale which served the White Horse. To find out if this service still operates phone 01768 870219.]

For walk 15
Services X4, 555 (all year) and 73 and X58 (seasonal) - Keswick to High Side

All the above services are operated by Stagecoach in Cumbria, telephone 0871 200 22 33. Buses depart from Keswick from Tithebarn Street opposite the Lakes supermarket, where timetables are displayed.

Bus Passes: One day, three day and seven day passes are purchasable on all buses. Their availability can considerably reduce the cost of bus travel in the Lake District for those visitors not in possession of a national bus pass.

Keswick Launch

This service is suggested for walks 10 and 12

The Keswick and Derwentwater Launch Company operates a launch service around Derwentwater calling at various points around the lake including Hawes End and Ashness. Operates all year round with greater frequency in the summer. For telephone enquiries phone 017687 72263

[NB. from Easter to October the Honister Rambler bus service 77/77A provides an alternative option to using the launch on walks 10 and 12.]

2012